D0938362

Nine O'Clock Coffee

Nine O'Clock Coffee

Poems
by
Bob Senseman

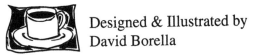 Designed & Illustrated by
David Borella

GOLDEN QUILL PRESS
Publishers Since 1902
Manchester Center, Vermont

Library of Congress Catalog
Card Number 95-078641

I.S.B.N. 0-8233-0503-1

Printed in the United States of America

This book
is dedicated
to our grandchildren who, as the ages
show, represent the hope & promise for
AMERICA .

ANDREW 10
CHRISTOPHER 7
KATHRYN 7
ERIC 6
DUNCAN 5
REID 3
STEPHANIE 3

March 1995

Special Thanks

PHIL RULON, Professor of History at Northern Arizona University and an author of many books, gave early and constant encouragement. His gentle criticism, often disguised as praise, was of great help.

DAVID BORELLA and I worked at the same company for many years and it has been rewarding and fun working with David again.

And, of course, my wife **BEE** has been a constant support and loving critic.

I am grateful to them and many others who have touched this book.

Contents

Nine O'Clock
Coffee

Nonsense

Ah yes
I'm a poet
I write words in rhyme
Some of the time
Then some of the time
I don't write in rhyme
Some of the time

> Ha Ha Ha
> Ho Ho Ho
> Hee Hee Hee

I'm overcome
By my own wit
But don't worry
I'll overcome it

Like I say
I'm a poet
I write words in rhyme
Some of the time
Then some of the time
I don't write in rhyme
Some of the time

Driving from Gallup
To Grants New Mexico
February 5 1994

Red rock bastions
Jut from mountain bases
Into the snow covered valley
Like ships in harbor
Pointing out to sea

On up the valley
Snow falls like sheets
On clothes lines
Stretched
From mountain top
To mountain top

Winter wind
Chases thin clouds
Down the mountain side
Mixing them
With the morning mist
The sun shines through
Forming mystic figures
Dancing
Around a sunlit fire
Chanting
"This land is ours"

To My Daughter in Denmark on Her 19th Birthday

The wind
Knocked on my door
And when I answered said let us fly
Let us explore
Earth and sky
Let your mind
Be mine
And see what treasures
We can find

We searched first
Among the trees
Whispering softly
To the leaves
Then dipping down
We touched the grass
Each blade bowed
As we passed
We gathered in
And moved along
Goldenrod seeds
And wild bird songs
I thrilled
At all within my view
I laughed
I cried
I thought of you

We rippled through
The field of wheat
Basking in the noonday's heat
Then passed along
The old fence row
Where bittersweet
And berries grow
Rushed down the hill
To the stream
To see diamonds dance
In golden beams
I saw myself in pools of blue
I smiled
I smiled
And thought of you

Resting then
We spent the hours
Nestled deep
Among wild flowers
Awaking kissed
Their tender blooms
And stole from them
Their choice perfumes
Mixed them
With the musky air
To form delights
Both real and rare
Beauty reigned
In form and hue
And beauty turned
My thoughts to you

Leaving beauty
We went our way
To search and find
Kids at play
Loud laughter
Filled the air
And filled the hearts
Of folks who care
We carried laughter
Down the street
To the park
Where lovers meet
And when the hush
Of evening drew
Silently
I thought of you

The wind
Like wind
Yearned to roam
It said good-bye
As I went home
We had shared a day
Just us two
The wind and I
With thoughts of you
In goldenrod
And bittersweet
In birds
And lovers so discreet

In the beauty
Of a single flower
In a rushing stream
And a silent hour
In kids
And clouds
And growing grain
You were there
To see
To be
With me
Again

Nine O'Clock Coffee
at The Weatherford Hotel

"I don't like it
And I won't vote for it"
Malcolm has arrived
At the Weatherford
For nine o'clock coffee
And he is stating his case
Against revitalization
Of downtown Flagstaff

Ten or eleven other guys
Are sitting around tables
Pushed together
To accommodate
Twenty or more
Who frequent the Weatherford
Every morning

The Weatherford
Is located downtown
And Sam and Henry
Are restoring it with loving care
It has its strong points
Charly's restaurant
A great wood-burning fireplace
Old bare-brick walls
And a print of the Grand Canyon painting
Commissioned to memorialize
Arizona's statehood in 1912

Counting myself
Twenty two guys showed up today
During the next thirty minutes
Everyone will chip in
With their two cents worth
And drink three cups
Of Charly's good coffee
At 9:30 Henry will rattle his spoon
In a white china soup bowl
And the "who pays" game will start

These guys are throwbacks
Fifty seventy ninety years old
Some retired
Some still in business
Some widowers
Some fat
Some bald
Some both

Throwback guys

All are fiercely independent
They despise government interference
Whether it's local
State or Federal
Taxation is a sin
Exceeded only by regulation
Yet most served in World War II or Korea
And would serve again if need be
They have served and are serving
As Councilmen
And community and church leaders
Few others have given as much of themselves

Throwback guys

Most
Grew up in the depression
In poverty as deep as hell
Some worked for the WPA
All worked at tough labor
Some went to college
Some didn't
Yet all are well-read
All keep up-to-date
All have been and are successful

Throwback Guys

Henry just rattled the spoon
And just in time
Pete and Malcolm were getting noisy
Which is useless on Pete's part
Malcolm never changes his mind

Yesterday John "won" the game
And paid for coffee
He runs the game today
He has recorded a secret number
Between 0 and 1,000
And decides to start the guessing game
Going around the table to the right
Because Jim Irby
Is eleven guesses away
And everyone wants to stick Irby

The guy on John's right
Starts the guessing
     "897"
     "High" says John
The next guy guesses
     "375"
     "High"
     "175"
     "Low"
So John's number
Is between 175 and 375

Bruce hits in the middle
    "275"
    "Low"
Still six guesses from Irby
    "325"
    "Low"
Now the chipping starts
    "360"
    "High"
    "344"
    "Low"
Mike asks
If there is any significance
To the number
John allows there is
But he isn't telling
Back to Mike
    "352"
    "Low"
Just two more guesses
And it's Irby's turn
    "354"
    "Low"
Joe takes the middle
    "357"
    "Low"

Irby can only guess
358 or 359
He makes appropriate comments
About blood suckers
Who needs enemies
Why me
And lets it fly
     "358"
     "Low"
Twenty one guys
Say "damn it" in unison
Irby dodges the bullet again
And Martin wins by default

Martin also makes appropriate
But perhaps stronger comments
No one listens
He pays for the coffee
The rest of us chip two bits
Into a bowl for a tip
And the group quickly disperses
I linger over my fourth cup
To reflect

Throwback guys

University President
Two auto dealers
Scientist
Librarian
Park Superintendent
Rancher
Astronomer
Insurance executives
Dentist
Small business entrepreneurs
College professors

Throwback guys

Back to when
Men were men
When men spoke more freely
Served more willingly
Loved more deeply
And lived more fully

Throwback guys

For about five minutes
I look into my black coffee
Thinking
Then absent mindedly
I toss another quarter into the bowl
And walk out

No Longer Brave

He stood there
Erect
Polished
Expectant
He was about to receive a high honor
And he was proud

He looked at the General
Who made the presentation
And he listened
But did not see or hear
It was obvious to all
That his was a body whole
With a soul that was broken

He took the Medal
With a steady hand
It was a brave sacrifice
His son had made
To earn the highest honor
His country bestowed

He turned to leave
He held the Medal
In his hand
And the dreams
For his son
In his heart

The Medal was bright
And shiny and real
His dreams were shattered
He bowed his head
And he cried

Fall

The trees unfurl
Their flags
Of red and orange
Whole hillsides
Parade in full dress
And the sun salutes

Geese
Trumpet taps for summer
The drumbeat of winter
Rolls by
On gusts of chilling winds
Fall
Marches through the Ozarks

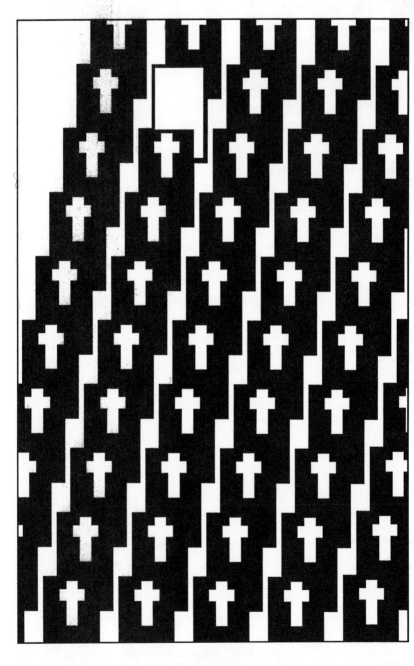

D-Day *June 6, 1994*

The stars are shining brightly
The night is crisp and moonless
Soon the morning
Will creep into the darkness
My army is ready
Even by star light
I can see the rows of men
Stretching endlessly into the valley
My steed is saddled
My sword is in its scabbard
This day will be
A grand and glorious day
For battle

These soldiers are trained by experience
Confident
Loyal
Capable
Courageous
The best our country has to offer
They are armed with mighty swords
And wear protective breastplates
And I must lead them to victory

As I ride back and forth
In front of this magnificent army
I am enthralled
By the straightness of the lines
In the dim light
Each soldier
Looks like every other soldier

I talk to my men
I tell them
We are fighting
For freedom
For our children
For our country
And I shout to them
Now is the time to advance
I turn my steed toward the enemy
And gallop forward
But when I look back at our lines
They are not advancing
They are motionless
In perfect alignment

I rein my steed
And return to confront my army
Why do they not follow
How can this great army
Not relish battle

This time
I appeal to their sense of duty
I stress the urgency of the moment
The need for surprise
That comes only at daybreak
Then I wheel and head for battle
But once again they do not follow

I return
Daylight is with us now
I can see the breastplate
On each soldier
With the soldier's name inscribed
I dismount
Hoping to entreat
The first man in each row
To follow me
They do not look at me
Or utter a word
As I go row to row
Reading the breastplates

    Row 1
        Sergeant John Bruener
        Died June 6 1944

    Row 2
        Corporal David Barken
        Died June 6 1944

    Row 3
        Lieutenant Allen O'Day
        Died June 6 1944

    Row 4
        Master Sergeant Robert Norris
        Died June 6 1944

    Row 5
        Captain Paul Rankin
        Died June 6 1944

There are many more rows
But it is useless to continue
I remount
And move slowly between two rows
To the place of a missing soldier

Dismounting
I unsaddle my steed
Slap him goodbye
And lie down
In my warm and peaceful coffin

To continue to dream

The dream of the dead

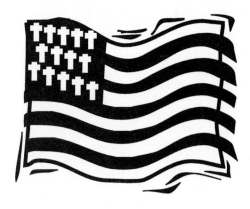

Standing Tall

The giant saguaros
Raise their arms
In praise
And thanks to God
For enabling them
To stand tall
To overcome
The extremes of nature
And enjoy
The beauty
Wonder
And drama
Of the Sonoran desert

The Psalm of Creation

I am standing in a ridge pasture
On my farm in Osage County Missouri
It is midnight on a moonless night
A few hours ago
The cows settled down
At the edge of the woods
With the wary deer and turkey nearby

Dusk-to-dawn lights
Strung along country roads
Are swallowed by the darkness
Like the dark sky swallows the stars
The night is brisk
And calm
And still
Nothing disturbs the tranquility
Except the presence of God

He breathes life into the air I breathe
His energy surges through my blood and fiber
He shakes my soul
He fires my mind
I feel myself
A part of the universe
I sense its strength
Its magic
Its order
I am at once alive and dead
I am everything and nothing
I am lost in the vastness
Of time and space

Somehow
Some way
I feel the forces
That have ordered the universe
For innumerable yesterdays
And will order it for innumerable tomorrows
Order
Absolute order
Each star in its place
Each star tugging at all other stars
All other stars tugging at each star
All in motion
All static
Absolute order
The order of the Universe

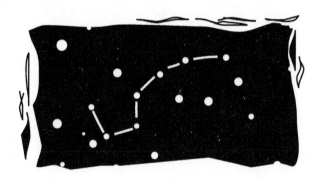

Psalm 148
1 Praise the Lord
  Praise the Lord from the heavens
  Praise Him in the heights
2 Praise Him all His angels
  Praise Him all His hosts
3 Praise Him sun and moon
  Praise Him all you shining stars
4 Praise Him you highest heavens
  And you waters above the heavens
5 Let them praise the name of the Lord
  For He commanded and they were created
6 And He established them forever and ever
  He fixed their bounds which cannot be passed

Come come Copernicus and Galileo
Come Plank and Newton
Come Einstein and Hawking
Join me at this magical moment
Feel the creation
Sense its simplicity
Marvel at its mystery

      Help me
      Help me

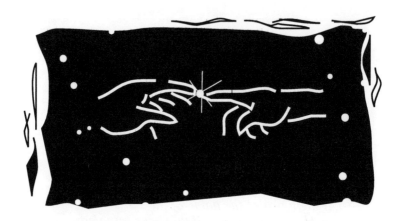

How did the universe begin
How will it end
Was the universe
Created from the dust
Of an earlier universe
Gathered together in a black hole
And rocketed forth with a big bang
To live again

Was the big bang
God's creation
Or a monumental accident
Wouldn't an all powerful God
Use all of His power
To create the order and magic
Of the universe
Wasn't the big bang
Surely the work
Of an even bigger God

All of you have struggled
To find a theory or equation
That explains all
Unifies all
Orders all
All to no avail
More knowledge leads to more unknowns
That lead to Cosmological Constants
The Uncertainty Principle
The Exclusion Principle
That lead to theories and equations
That in the end do not equate

       Help me
       Help me

Perhaps
If there is no Creator
There is no equation of unification
How can happenstance
Be expressed mathematically
Perhaps
If there is a Creator
There is a set of laws
That orders our universe
But if the Creator
Fixed the bounds of the stars
Is he bound to reveal the fix

At the instant
Before the big bang
At the beginning of time
Were all four forces
Gravitational
Electro-magnetic
Weak nuclear
Strong nuclear
Were all four forces
Unified in the hands of God
Isn't it probable
That the theory you seek
Is still in the hands of God
Isn't it probable
The mystery of the Creation
Will always defy man
The Creator's noblest creation

Psalm 8
3 When I look at the heavens
  The work of your fingers
  And the stars which thou has established
4 What is man
  That thou are mindful of him
  And the son of man
  That thou dost care for him

Come Gautama and Confucius
Come Aristotle and Socrates
Come Jesus and Paul
Come Mohammed
Join us at this magical moment
Feel the Creation
Sense its simplicity
Marvel at its mystery

      Help me
      Help me

Which of you knows
The Grand Unification Theory of Life
That explains all
Unifies all
Orders all
That connects the murderer
To the victim
Man to Woman
Life to Death
Are the forces that order matter
The same for life
I am made
Of the same stuff as the stars
I am atoms
Protons
Quarks
I am matter
And I live to be swept up
By the black hole of death
To live again

If the order of the universe
Is accidental
Is my life ordered just as accidentally
Or has an all-powerful Creator
Fixed the bounds of life
And not revealed the fix

Is it possible that the four forces
Were not the only creations
Of the big bang
Perhaps at that instant
Every idea
Every thought
Everything metaphysical
Was created too
Good and evil
Mind and soul
Love and hate
Forgiveness
Everything
Including the Holy Spirit
The fifth force
Carrying God's power
To every nook and cranny
Of space

And then God left his Creation
In the hands of time
Time for man
To spring from the dust
That housed his genetic trace
Time for mankind to seek its destiny
Aided and abetted by the Holy Spirit
God had created paths to heaven
And to hell
It was up to man and to woman
To choose the paths they wanted to follow

Help me
Help me

Psalm 102
25 Of old thou didst lay
   The foundations of the earth
   And the heavens
   Are the work of thy hands
26 They will perish
   But thou dost endure
   They will all wear out
   Like a garment
27 But thou art the same
   And thy years have no end

Is it possible
In limitless time
That the universe and man
Will be recreated by God
Again and again
But ordered differently
Until man and God
Become as one
Dwelling in God's Perfect Universe

     Help me
     Help me

Which of you
Has the answers
Which of you
Has held the hand of God

Hush
Hush

I hear a sure voice

"I was
 I am
 I will be"

Psalm 148
7 Praise the Lord from the Earth
  You sea monsters and all deeps
8 Fire and hail snow and frost
  Stormy wind fulfilling his command
9 Mountains and all hills
  Fruit trees and all cedars
10 Beasts and all cattle
  Creeping things and flying birds
11 Kings of the earth and all peoples
  Princes and rulers of the earth
12 Young men and maidens together
  Old men and children
13 Let them praise the name of the Lord
  For His name alone is exalted
  His glory is above earth and heaven

It's getting light now
The deer are coming into the field
The cattle are stirring
        There is work to do
        I must help

Childlike Innocence

The little boy
Playing in the decay
Of an old tree stump
Watched the line of ants
Disappear into the rubble
Then stamped the last two
With his foot
And wondered why the two ants
Didn't follow the others
And in childlike innocence
He cried

A few years later
The boy shot a sparrow
As it fluttered to the ground
He searched for another
And shouted for joy
As it too tumbled from the tree

In time
The guns and game
Grew larger
As did the boy
In full manhood
He hunted and killed
Exotic and rare specimens
All over the world
And mounted them
In his den
For his pleasure
To his friends
He gave rugs and hangings
From the excess game
He enjoyed hunting and killing

      Now the boy
      Is a doddering old man
      Day after day
      He sits in his den
      With his guns in the case
      Unable to remember
      When or how
      The musty animals around him
      Were killed

      He wonders why
      They can't join their kind
      Unaware
      That the jungles plains and mountains
      From which they came
      Are no longer habitats
      For game or hunter
      And in childlike innocence
      He cries

On A Clear Night

When I walk
On a clear night
I see stars
Blinking their codes
Of beauty
And light
Like candles on a Christmas tree

And I wonder
How can some stars
Blink tonight
Yet be cold and lifeless in star-world
What power
Keeps the star-candle blinking
After the candle burns out

When I lay in bed
I wonder
What is my life about
What will it be about
When I'm gone

Does my life shine brightly
Like candles on a Christmas tree
Will my life-candle
Still have power
To blink its codes
Of love
And hope
And inspiration
Long after the candle burns out

Poem For The Day

Little toy soldiers
Gather dust
Along the wall
Red fire engine
Is in the corner
Next to a big blue ball
Santa Claus has come and gone
But Barry
Like most little boys
Is still content
With a cardboard box
And yesterday's well-worn toys

Ghosts and Ghouls

I draw the shades
On yesterday
Yet plainly I can see
Ghosts and Ghouls
Of errant ways
Parade in front of me
I raise the shades
On the 'morrow
And much to my surprise
Ghosts and Ghouls
Tears and sorrow
Greet my troubled eyes

The past never seems
To walk with me
To keep me on the path
I look but never seem to see
Tomorrow's fears
Tomorrow's wrath
Where is the peace
That comes with age
Where is the still still voice
That calms and soothes
Internal rage
And circumscribes my choice

The voice is there
I do not hear
Its plea to slow the pace
Voices dear
Shout calls more clear
That keep me in the race

Heaven is for those
Who join the fray
The bold who know full well
That Ghosts and Ghouls
Of timid ways
Lead to the gates of hell

An Old Dead Owl

By chance the other day
I found an old dead owl
To my dismay
Predators
Had picked an eye away
One leg was gone
And a wing was broken
It was beautiful
That old dead owl
Was beautiful

Don't ask me how
An old dead owl
With one eye
And one leg
And a broken wing
Can be beautiful
It was grotesque
Even hideous
But it was beautiful
That old dead owl
Was beautiful

I asked a passerby
To look at the old dead owl
I said
"Isn't it beautiful"
He didn't say a word
But with wary eye
And quickened step
He told me
That I must be sick
Or dazed
Or crazed
To think an old dead owl
With one eye
And one leg
And a broken wing
Is beautiful
He was gone

I looked at the owl
And brushed a maggot away
Two feathers fell from his broken wing
I picked the owl up softly
And took it to a friend
I said
"Look at this old dead owl
With one eye
One leg
And a broken wing
Isn't it beautiful"

My friend looked at the owl
And said he couldn't see how an old dead owl
Could be dead
And beautiful
Especially
When the owl had laid
Outside
And of course decayed
"The owl is dead
It's rotten
It stinks"
My friend said
"And it's not beautiful"
"Of course the owl is dead"
I said
"How could an old owl
With one eye
And one leg
And a broken wing
Be alive and beautiful
The owl is beautiful
Because it's dead"
My friend turned
And walked away

And so
As it was getting late
I took the old dead owl
To the tree
Where he had often hooted
For his mate
Choosing a spot
Where the sun
Would warm his grave
I dug that grave
And gently buried the old dead owl
With one eye
And one leg
And a broken wing

Holding his head high
I arranged his wings
As best I could
To reflect his pride
Then I placed
The easy warm dirt
Around him like a blanket
Tamping it down
To form a crown
For his grave

I found an old board
And on it carved
These simple words
"An old dead owl"
And placed it on the grave
Stepping back a pace
I said a prayer and said good-bye
To that old dead owl
With one eye
One leg
And a broken wing
Then with tears
Streaming down my face
I turned and walked away
From that old dead owl's
Final resting place

Charlie

The town looked down on Charlie
He never went to school
They called him Charlie-What's-His-Name
They said he was a fool
Charlie walked the river's banks
Fools have nothing else to do
He talked to birds and animals
They talked to Charlie too

When Charlie went to Viet Nam
Not a tear was shed
They say that Charlie's coming back
They say that Charlie's dead
They're going to have a big parade
A military band
For Charlie died a hero's death
In good old Viet Nam

All the people in the town
Have gone to church to pray
Businesses have closed their doors
To celebrate the day
The mayor will make a speech
Extolling Charlie's fame
And they'll dedicate a monument
To Charlie-What's-His-Name

The trees all stand in hushed array
The birds forget their song
Fox and deer weep near the path
That Charlie walked along
The river wears a veil of tears
It's him the weeping's for
The fool who walked the river's banks
Walks those banks no more

Searching

The young sweetheart
Torn apart
By war from her lover
With tearful eye
And muffled cry
Searched the sky above her

She couldn't see
For he couldn't be
But long she stayed to stare
She drew a sigh
From the azure sky
For he had flown there

On Violence

Computers
All shapes
All sizes
Different features
Different powers
Different makes
Assimilate
Data
Program
Data
Spit out
Facts
On screen
On paper

Facts
No better
Than
Input
Or program
That
Sifts
Sorts
Spits
Sign on the wall
Garbage in
Garbage out

Young mind
Supercomputer
Great capacity
Quick
Creative
Alert
Sucks up
Sights
Sounds
Situations
Spits out
Acts
At home
On streets

Acts
No better
Than
Input
Sights
Sounds
Situations
TV
Guns
Blood
Sex
Murder
Sign on the wall
Violence in
Violence out

The Creature

A large crowd
Perhaps 100,000 or more
Gathered in the streets
And on the sidewalks
To catch a glimpse
Of The Creature

I could hear faintly
The big sound truck
Far down the street
Just beyond the park
As it approached
I could hear
The blaring creature lyrics
Lyrics full of expletives
And sex
And violence
The young crowd seemed thrilled
Shouting the same expletives
That roared from the sound truck
They were becoming impatient
To see the Creature

And soon he came
With motorcycle police
In front
On each side
And in back
Of the giant wheeled platform
That carried the Creature and his entourage

Interspersed with the police
Were rolling TV crews
Each hoping to get
The best coverage for the nightly news
Some stations would bleep the lyrics
To allow their reports
To include music
By the Creature

The recorded music became silent
The Creature was live now
He started with
The least offensive lyrics
But soon
Encouraged by shouts from the crowd
Launched into those lyrics
That had made him famous
Songs full of moral destruction
Laced not with suggestive phrases
Of love and romance
But rather with
Explicit sexual descriptions
Reinforced by equally explicit gyrations
And the crowd loved it
Responding as if in a trance
Swaying back and forth
And gyrating in concert with
The Creature

I too fell into a trance
To me
The Creature looked like a creature
His hair was dirty and unruly
His appearance
Like that of a wild animal
His skin a putrid green
And to my amazement
The crowd was taking on
The animal-like countenance
Of the Creature

I was so deep in a trance
That I hardly noticed
A well-dressed gentleman
Tugging at my clothing
As I took note of him
I realized that he was talking to me
I became irritated
As he deplored
The actions of the crowd
And implored me
To stop following the Creature

Finally I could no longer tolerate
His nagging and pleading
I turned on him and shouted
"You son-of-a-bitch
If you don't like the Creature
Get the hell out of here"
The crowd cheered
And shouted its approval
And the well-dressed gentleman
Disappeared as if by magic

For sometime
The crowd continued to recognize me
I was exhilarated and excited
I quickened my pace down the sidewalk
Following the Creature
As closely as the police would allow

And then
I saw my reflection
In a plate-glass window
It was devastating
I too had dirty and unruly hair
I too looked like a wild animal
I too had putrid green skin
Like the rest of the crowd
I too was Creature

I took a few more steps
Then stopped
I could feel my heart
My mind
My soul
My self
Leaving me
I was exhausted

I stood there
Numb
As the crowd rushed by
Then I turned
And walked slowly in the opposite direction
Looking for the well-dressed gentleman
But he was gone

I walked on down the street to the park
And sat on a bench
Too weary to continue
Too ashamed to go home
After what seemed an eternity
I felt a tap on my shoulder
It was the well-dressed gentleman
He sat down beside me
And we talked late into the night
And then he disappeared
Again as if by magic

I continued
To sit on the bench
Thinking
Contemplating the wisdom
Of the well-dressed gentleman
Gradually I regained my composure
As the day broke
I went home

At Chesterfield's Bar

Come Come
My boys
Lift the cup
Cheers to all
Bottoms up
Tomorrow's fears
Are far away
When they come
It will be
Today

Hic

Man And Battle

I

You
Down in the trench
Down in the foxhole
How does the stench
Of burning powder
Screaming shells ever louder
How does war affect you

What is it like
To sleep
Next to a dead man
Or do you sleep
Or cover your head
And silently weep
Weep
Weep
There is no shame
There is no loss of pride
There are fears man cannot conceal
Emotions he cannot hide

But why are you weeping
Is that man lying there still
That man eternally sleeping
Worse off than you
How could he be
Look what you face
Rain
Mud
Bullets
Unknown misery
While lying there he is serene
He's found his resting place

What is it in you
What do you possess
That you heed not
The burst of screaming shells
Or shrapnel's deadly rattle
But bravely face hell
And plunge headlong into battle

Brave
No man is brave
We all are cowards
You as much as I
Yet I doubt that I could charge
If I know I were to die
And know you must
You cannot stay
Listening to the whine
Of well aimed missiles
Day by day
And trust
That when you leave your trench
They will not hit you
War is not that just

What manner are you men
Who face bullet after bullet
In battle after battle
And hope to live again

II

Flying men on lofty peaks
Never found before
Where bursting shells
And burning streaks
Dance around galore
Tell me please your story

You chase the fleeing enemy
In and out of clouds
Until his plane goes down in flame
And he trusts his life to shrouds
Does the stalk
The attack
The kill
The tensing of your nerves
Make this war a game of skill
A means to gain mere glory

You carefully
Adjust your sight
And cast your bombs away
And the target below
In the peaceful night
Is suddenly bright as day
While the people asleep on downy bed
Continue to sleep
For they are dead

Then you change the course
Of your winged steed
And head for home
With added speed
Does all this spectacle
Of fiery destruction
And flaming death
Does all this bloody gore
Cause a tear for every breath
Or add excitement to the war

Or is your plane a bed
That harbors the living dead
That man on your wing
Or you in fact
Might fall behind your group closely packed
And the enemy shall spot its prey
And this will be your final day
To go aloft in your armored mount
All the world below to flount
For you and the earth shall be as one
When the enemy finds the time
To clean the powder and the grime
From a true and trusty gun

What manner are you men
Who fly through bullets
Rockets
Flak
And hope beyond hope
That you will come back

III

And you
Who sail on and below
The surface of the seas
Who polish and practice
And practice and polish
To be ready
When the enemy comes into view
And the deep becomes a grave
For the enemy or you

What is there to this game of war
That you believe worth fighting for
When the bells clang the call to station
The polish and practice are over
You know the enemy
Polishes and practices too
You know the bells clang on his ship
You know that he has been hunting you

And now you see
The smoke from his guns
And feel the surge of power
As your ship maneuvers
To be sure this is the hour
Of victory
The heat
The fear
The noise
The smoke
Create hell
Why in all the din
Do you thing you will win
Are you so busy
That you don't know
That both the weak and the brave
Will end the battle in a watery grave

What manner are you men
Who with every heartbeat
Every breath
Think only the enemy
Will end the day
In death

IV

In all the fear
And horror of war
Man doesn't act
As he has before
Each grim and dangerous task
Is done
No questions asked
Why
Where does man acquire
The spark
That's whipped
Into a fire
Is it a patriot's love
Or his own desire

Author's Notes

Nine O'Clock Coffee at the Weatherford Hotel
I look forward to my coffee in the morning at the
Weatherford Hotel. This coffee gang knows how to
disagree without being disagreeable. We discuss
serious subjects and my thoughts on some of those
subjects are expressed in poems included in this book.
The poem, while hopefully entertaining, has it's
serious side too. The seemingly vanishing male role
in American family life is accentuated by the strict
adherence to that role by my coffee cohorts.

The Psalm of Creation
I have read and studied Hawking's book, *A Brief
History of Time*, and am familiar with the Biblical
explanation of the Creation. I have spent many hours
at night alone on a hill trying to resolve in my mind the
scientific and Biblical explanations. The Psalm of
Creation, written in a period encompassing 1991, '92,
and '93, results from those hilltop experiences.

D-Day June 6 1994

On June 6, 1994 the media replayed the films and recounted the heroism and sacrifices of those involved in D-Day 1944. Along with most Americans I honored those who lost their lives and those who lived through the beginning of the end of World War II. During that day of remembrance I wondered...what would those who died on June 6, 1944 say if they could talk. The poem was written that day as a possible answer.

Old Dead Owl

In the late seventies, I began contemplating my mother's death but found it impossible to write about my feelings. One day when my thoughts seemed focused on that inevitable happening, I wrote An Old Dead Owl. Mother lived until 1991...she was a beautiful woman even when she died at the age of 92 after a long illness. The viewing at the funeral home and my grief at the grave site are aptly described in the poem written ten years before her death.

Charlie
A I am writing these notes, the United States is reliving the Vietnam War on the 20th Anniversary of its ending. Charlie was written in 1969 reflecting my criticism of the hypocritical way our leaders conducted the war and the hypocrisy of the general public, too. Secretary of Defense Robert S. McNamara's book, just released, verifies that hypocrisy.

Creature
Great law and great thoughts are incorporated in words that are derivations or extensions of the word "civil"...civilian...civility...civil rights...civil liberties. Yet a rapidly growing number of Americans at all levels of income and education are speaking and acting in less civil ways. Who is at fault? Creature, written in 1994, deals with that question.

Man and Battle
I am very interested in the concept of war and the thoughts of those involved in war. Why is war necessary in a civilized society? Why are human beings capable of killing other human beings? Recently, some attention is being given to the possibility that the desire to fight (as in a war) ...may be inbred...a part of our psyche.
Man and Battle was written in 1946.